# THE YOUNG SCIENTIST BOOK OF MEDICINE DOCTORS AND H...

**Pam Beasant**
**Designed by Iain Ashman**

Edited by Tony Potter
Consultant editor Dr. Gillian Strube
Consultants Drs. Val and Mike Patton

## Contents

Illustrated by Iain Ashman, Adam Willis, Stuart Trotter, Chris Lyon, Martin Newton, Michael Saunders, Gerry Browne, Tony Smith and Mark Longworth

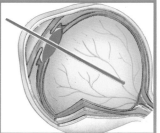

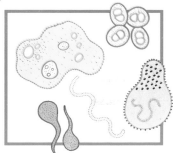

# What is medicine?

Medicine is the study of how the body is cured when it goes wrong, how it is kept healthy and how illness is prevented. On these two pages you can find out about the subject of medicine.

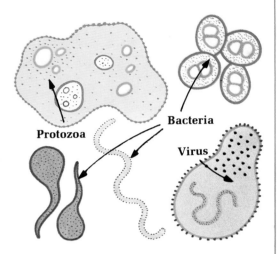

Protozoa

Bacteria

Virus

People become ill for many reasons. Mostly it is because germs invade their bodies and multiply. Some of these germs are shown above and you can find out more about them on pages 8-9.

Many diseases in the past spread because people lived in unsanitary conditions in crowded houses where germs spread very quickly.

Modern sewage works

The development of sewage systems and the supply of clean drinking water have done more than anything else to improve the health of everybody.

Over the last fifty years, medicine has become a sophisticated science using techniques and equipment which are sometimes borrowed from other fields, such as space research. Laser surgery, for instance, uses concentrated beams of light to cut through the skin cleanly during an operation.

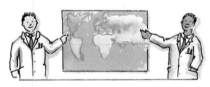

A laser beam being used in surgery.

Health and medicine are very different around the world because of factors such as climate, environment and food. You can find out about this on pages 26-27.

## What is the body made of?

When people study medicine, they first learn what the body is made of and how a healthy body works.

**1** Your entire body is made of billions of tiny units called cells. They work together all the time to keep it functioning properly.

**2** There are different kinds of cells, each with a different job to do; for instance red blood cells carry oxygen around your body and nerve cells send messages of sensation and pain to your brain.

A single skin cell

Red blood cells

Tissue

**3** Your body has layers of tissue, which are groups of cells of similar type, such as skin and muscle.

## Medical people

There are many different kinds of medical people including family doctors, specialists and different kinds of nurses. Midwives, for instance, are nurses who are experts at delivering babies. The picture on the right shows some of the main people involved with medicine. There are also people whose jobs take them into the field of medicine, such as epidemiologists (who study why outbreaks of disease happen) and health officers (who check the cleanliness of restaurants, for instance).

Doctor

Midwife

The specialist doctor in charge of a hospital unit is called a consultant.

Nurses work shifts to run hospital wards 24 hours a day.

Physio-therapists help people to move properly after an illness or accident.

When you become ill your body reacts by showing symptoms such as a headache, diarrhoea or vomiting. You can find out more about symptoms on the next two pages.

When you are ill you see a doctor who has a general knowledge of all types of illness. He or she decides what is wrong after examining you and asking lots of questions. This is called making a diagnosis – find out how it is done on pages 14-15.

Sterile (germ-free) clothing          Surgeon

The doctor will treat you according to the diagnosis – perhaps with pills or an injection, or you may be sent to hospital for tests or to be examined with a view to operating.

Acupuncture needles

Sometimes people prefer to have alternative forms of treatment for their illness. There are many different alternative therapies available, such as acupuncture, which has been practised for centuries in China. Find out about this on pages 18-19.

The doctor can prevent some illnesses by giving an injection which makes you resist them. This is called immunization – find out more about it on pages 12-13.

Vegetables

Bread          Fruit

Fish

You can also help to prevent illness yourself by eating a balanced diet and taking exercise.

4 It also has organs, which are groups of tissue. Your heart, liver, stomach and lungs are all examples of organs.

The heart is one of your main organs.

The blood system

5 Groups of organs which work together are called systems. Your heart and veins, for instance, make up your circulatory (blood) system which keeps the blood flowing round your body.

You also have a special system called the immune system which is a complicated mass of organs and chemicals whose job it is to fight illness. You can find out about this on pages 10-11.

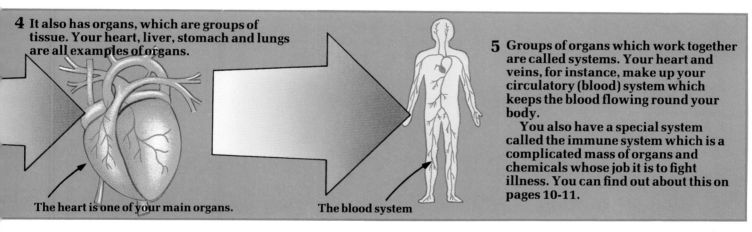

Speech therapist (see page 17).          Surgeon

Occupational therapists train people if they have been handicapped.

A radiologist is an expert in X-ray medicine.

Anaesthetists (an-ees-thetist) specialize in the drugs used to make patients unconscious during an operation.

Paediatricians (pee-dee-a-trishan) specialize in children's illnesses.

Medical scientists analyse samples and research new techniques for treating illness.

Specialists are experts on one part of the body or one group of illnesses. Each has a special name which is sometimes long and difficult to pronounce because it is taken from Latin. Cardiologists, for example, are experts on heart disease, and haematologists (hee-mo-tolo-jists) specialize in blood disorders. Many specialists work in hospitals, which are divided into units for each branch of medicine. Some travel to patients' homes to give treatment, and others work in clinics and health centres.

# About illness

Most illnesses are caused by tiny particles called germs coming into your body. These live off substances in cells which you need to keep healthy. You then start to feel ill because your body cannot function in its normal way.

Your body reacts when ill by showing symptoms such as a temperature, a cough or a headache. Each illness has its own particular combination of symptoms which is how you or a doctor knows what is wrong with you. On these two pages, you can find out how your body reacts to illness.

## Germs

Germs live in your body all the time, are present in the food you eat and are also in the air. Most of them are harmless. Germs multiply in most places, but prefer warm, damp or

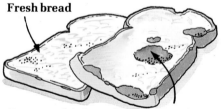

Fresh bread

Germs multiply making the bread mouldy.

dirty conditions. When certain germs multiply in food, the food goes bad and when they multiply in you they can cause illness. There are many kinds of germs and you can find out about them on pages 8-9.

## Your defences

Your body is prepared for an invasion, or infection, of germs and starts to fight them immediately. This is done by a network of organs* and chemicals called the immune system which destroy and control germs.

Your immune system will recognize an illness you have had before, such as measles. It will fight the germs and kill them off before they have any effect.

Immune system

Germs

THE BODY

Germs recognized and killed.

THIS WAY

4

*See page 3.

## Before the symptoms

Most illnesses take some time to secure their hold on the body. This is called the incubation period and can vary from a few days to several months. When it is finished, the symptoms of the illness appear.

This person has caught 'flu (influenza) but feels fine.

Two days later the symptoms start.

Follow the squares on the board to find out how illness develops and how your body reacts by showing symptoms.

## Being sick

Being sick, or vomiting, is caused by a number of things from food poisoning to over-eating. Whatever the reason for being sick, however, the same things are going on inside your body when it happens.

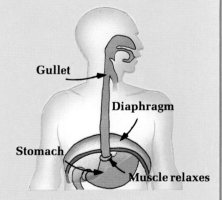

Gullet

Diaphragm

Stomach

Muscle relaxes

When you are sick, the lining of your stomach becomes irritated, making your stomach contract violently at the same time as the muscle at the end of your gullet relaxes. Your diaphragm also contracts, pushing against your stomach and forcing everything in it up your throat and out of your mouth.

## Diarrhoea

Diarrhoea is when all the solid waste inside the bowel becomes runny and liquid. It is usually caused by a stomach upset, such as food poisoning. Food does not go through the normal digestion processes, and only a little is absorbed by the body. Diarrhoea causes a loss of liquid, so as much water as possible should be drunk to make up for it.

VOMITING

You eat some bad food

START

HEADACHE

Stay in bed for a day

Feeling marvellous – go to a party

Friend has measles

## Headache

A headache is caused by pressure around your brain. The pain is caused by the blood vessels in your brain contracting then expanding. A headache can happen for many reasons. It may be due to an infection, or because the muscles in your neck and scalp become tense.

Normal size blood vessels.

Expanded blood vessels causing a headache.

## Sneezing

Sneezing is your body's way of getting rid of anything irritating your nose. A cold, for instance, makes the inside of your nose inflamed and you sneeze to relieve it. If you are allergic* to anything, such as pollen, then you will sneeze to get rid of pollen particles in your nose.

## Coughing

Coughing is called a reflex action which means that your body does it automatically. You cannot help coughing if you breathe in dust, or choke on food. Coughing stops anything from getting into your lungs and makes you swallow or spit it out instead. If you have a cold, for instance, mucus builds up in your air passages, and you cough to get rid of it.

## How blood defends you

Blood contains red cells and white cells. The red cells carry oxygen around your whole body and make your blood look red. There are fewer white cells, but they are a very important part of your body's defence system. If you cut yourself, lots of red and white blood cells go to the area and the white cells eat any germs that may be getting into the cut. There are also particles called platelets in blood which help it to clot. This is why a cut always stops bleeding after a while.

White blood cell

A germ being destroyed by a white blood cell.

Sometimes cuts or spots become infected by germs. When this happens pus forms. Pus is made of dead white blood cells which gather in the area round the cut or spot. The more germs that enter the area, the greater the number of white cells that go into action. It is better to leave a small cut uncovered as this allows a dry crust called a scab to form which also protects the cut from germs.

Dead white blood cells forming pus in a cut.

Feeling run down

Meet someone with a cold

DIARRHOEA

Develop cold

SNEEZE AND COUGH

HEALTHY AGAIN

TEMPERATURE

Getting better

RASH

Develop measles

## Temperature

Your normal body temperature, even in cold weather, is 37°C (98.4°F). Having a temperature means that your body temperature has gone higher than this.

39°C    Thermometer

This is a high temperature.

A temperature is often caused by an infection such as 'flu. When the 'flu germs damage healthy cells, they release certain chemicals which make you feel feverish and hot.

## Rash

A rash is a skin irritation caused by an infection or allergy. For example, when you have measles, tiny blood vessels in your skin called capillaries, are damaged and release chemicals which cause a rash. The damaged capillaries cause an increase in blood to the skin, making it look red.

Normal capillary

Swollen capillary causing a red rash.

## What is pain?

Pain is a symptom of illness because your body is telling you there is something wrong with it.

Pain is part of the system inside you which responds to touch, taste and smell (called the sensory system). Tiny fibres, called nerves, send messages to your brain when something is painful. Your brain identifies the site, and sometimes the cause of the pain.

Pain message going to brain.

Nerve ending, or receptor.

A sharp leaf.

Skin

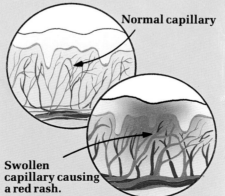

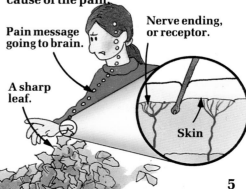

*An allergy is an abnormal reaction to normally harmless substances.

5

# Things that go wrong with the body

Although many illnesses are caused by germs, there are lots of other reasons why people become ill. For example, babies can be born with an illness inherited from their parents.

On these two pages, you can find out about some of the main kinds of illnesses there are. On pages 8-9 you can find out about infections – the germs that cause them and how they spread.

## Blood circulation disorders

Blood circulates constantly in the body, pumped by the heart. It carries oxygen which every cell, organ and system in the body needs to function. Oxygen is distributed from the lungs to main blood vessels (arteries) and from there to small arteries, then to small blood vessels (capillaries) and then to cells. Many diseases arise from the blood-flow being obstructed, which restricts the oxygen supply. This can result in reactions ranging from a faint to a heart attack (see opposite).

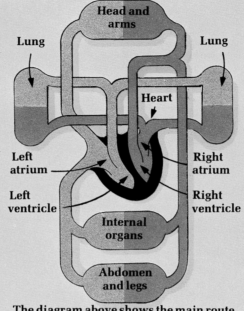

The diagram above shows the main route of the blood through the heart and round the body.

A pacemaker is a battery-powered electrical generator, inserted into the chest and attached to the heart with a fine wire. It regulates the beat of a heart not pumping properly.

Wire to heart

### Heart disease

Heart disease is a disorder in the main arteries on the surface of the heart (coronary arteries). It happens because a fatty substance called cholesterol is deposited inside the arteries making them narrower and narrower, restricting the blood-flow. Heart disease is not necessarily dangerous in itself, but it can lead to a heart attack, or a condition called angina which gives the sufferer acute chest pains after exercise.

### Heart attacks

A heart attack is a lack of blood to the heart causing it to spasm. It happens for various reasons. There might be a blood clot in one of the coronary arteries, for instance, or a narrow segment of diseased artery might suddenly spasm. A heart attack causes severe chest pains and sometimes the person collapses. Anyone who suffers a heart attack, even a minor one, should be taken to hospital.

### Strokes

A stroke is the result of an interruption of the blood supply to parts of the brain. This deprives the cells of oxygen and means they cannot work properly. These are usually the cells that control movement, speech and vision. In many cases people who have had a stroke lose some or all of these faculties for a while, but wholly or partially recover them after a few months. In severe cases, however, the sufferer can be left handicapped or die.

## Industrial diseases

Industrial diseases affect workers in mines, chemical plants, factories and anywhere where there is a risk of breathing in excessive amounts of dust or chemical pollution over a number of years. They are usually diseases of the lung and respiratory systems. Miners, for example, often suffer from forms of bronchitis through breathing in coal dust which has been circulating in stale underground air. You can find out more about industrial diseases and how they affect health and the environment on pages 26-27.

Workers are given chest X-rays routinely in some factories containing a high level of dust.

## Cancer

In general, cancer refers to the uncontrolled division and spread of faulty cells in the body, which destroy healthy cells. The disease can take many forms – it can cause growths called malignant tumours, for example. It can start in any part of the body. The pictures below show sections of two lungs – one with healthy cells and one with cancerous cells. People who smoke are much more likely to develop lung cancer. Many forms of cancer are now treated successfully, as long as they are spotted before they start to spread to other areas of the body.

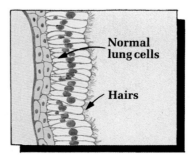

Normal lung cells

Hairs

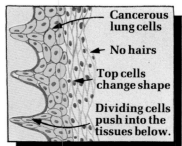

Cancerous lung cells

No hairs

Top cells change shape

Dividing cells push into the tissues below.

# Hereditary diseases

Diseases can be inherited from parents in the same way that eye and hair colour is inherited from them. These are called hereditary diseases. The unborn child is formed in the mother's womb with the disease.

A disease called haemophilia is carried, but not suffered, by some women. They can pass it on to male children who actually suffer the disease. The blood of a haemophiliac boy does not clot easily and even a small cut can bleed dangerously.

A woman carrying haemophilia has a 1 in 4 chance of giving birth to a boy who suffers from the disease. Before looking at the chart which explains this, find out in the paragraphs on the right how a child is formed.

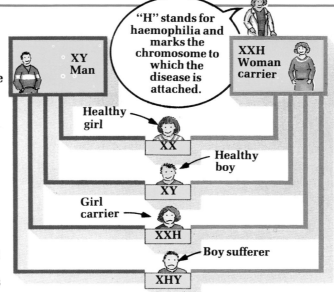

"H" stands for haemophilia and marks the chromosome to which the disease is attached.

XY Man

XXH Woman carrier

Healthy girl — XX

Healthy boy — XY

Girl carrier — XXH

Boy sufferer — XHY

A child is formed by two cells; an egg cell from its mother and a sperm cell from its father. A part called a sex chromosome from each cell determines the child's sex. An egg cell always gives an X chromosome and a sperm cell either an X or a Y chromosome. A girl is made from 2 X chromosomes and a boy from an X and a Y chromosome.

Haemophilia is carried by one of the woman's X chromosomes.

# Illnesses needing surgery

Some illnesses are caused by infections in an organ, or growths in the body which cause obstructions. These illnesses can often be completely cured by surgery to remove the diseased tissue. Operations can also repair damaged veins, replace joints, remove blood clots and transplant organs that are faulty. A common illness needing surgery is appendicitis. You can find out about on the right .

Your appendix has no function in your body so you do not miss it if it is removed.

Large intestine

Small intestine

Appendix

Animals such as rabbits have a large appendix to help them digest grass.

### Appendicitis

Appendicitis happens when a small, tail-shaped part of the intestine, called the appendix, suddenly becomes swollen and infected. The appendix is at the end of the small intestine. Nobody knows why it should become infected.

An infected appendix is removed in hospital. On pages 20-21, you can find out how this operation is done. If the appendix is left it can burst, spreading infection through the intestines and leading to a dangerous illness called peritonitis.

# Deficiency diseases

Deficiency diseases happen because the body is lacking (deficient) in some of the things it needs. Mostly they are caused by poor diet but sometimes they happen because the body is unable to manufacture certain substances. A condition called iron-deficiency anaemia is caused by a lack of iron in the red blood cells. This can happen when people do not eat food which contain iron such as green vegetables.

## Malnutrition

Malnutrition is an extreme and preventable deficiency disease caused by inadequate nourishment of any kind. It is widespread in countries which do not have enough food for their inhabitants. Malnutrition affects the growth and development of the body, increasing the body's reaction to infection and lowering its resistance to germs.

## AIDS

AIDS stands for Acquired Immune Deficiency Syndrome. It is a serious disease which attacks the immune system, leaving the sufferer vulnerable to any infection and sometimes completely lacking in immunity or the ability to fight germs. Doctors do not yet know exactly what causes AIDS or how to treat it successfully.

About 15% of the world's population suffers from malnutrition. Two-thirds of these live in South East Asia.

AIDS can be transmitted sexually, and through blood transfused from a donor who has the disease.

# Iatrogenic diseases

Iatrogenic diseases are those caused by doctors, medicines and forms of treatment designed to cure illnesses. These diseases are not intended, but happen through the careless administration of medicines, or mistakenly diagnosing an illness, or through the side-effects of medicines given for another disorder.

In the early 1960s, a drug called thalidomide was given to some pregnant women to relieve morning sickness. It prevented the normal growth of limbs in some of the babies – a side-effect unforeseen by doctors and scientists.

People who receive radiotherapy for cancer often suffer nausea and hair-loss caused by the treatment.

# Infections

Infections are illnesses that spread from person to person. Mumps, measles, colds and 'flu are all examples. Infections are caused by four main kinds of germs. These are viruses, bacteria, protozoa and fungi. Germs are parasites, which means they live off healthy cells and multiply there. They move or are carried to the body in different ways and enter the body by several routes.

Here, you can find out about the germs that cause infections and how they spread.

## Viruses

Viruses are so small that they cannot be seen under an ordinary microscope. Different viruses cause illnesses such as colds, 'flu and chickenpox. The virus particles

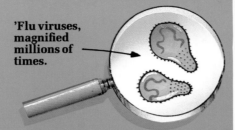

'Flu viruses, magnified millions of times.

burrow into healthy cells and live off them to produce more virus particles. The healthy cells die and the virus moves on through your body to find more cells to live off.

## Bacteria

Bacteria (singular bacterium) are tiny single-celled creatures found everywhere. They reproduce by dividing into two when they reach a certain size. This is called fission. Some can damage tissues in the body

Streptococcus causes sore throats.

These bacteria also have Latin names.

and produce poisonous chemicals which make you ill.

Some bacteria can be useful too. For example, one kind lives in humans and produces a substance called vitamin K which helps blood to clot.

## How germs get into the body

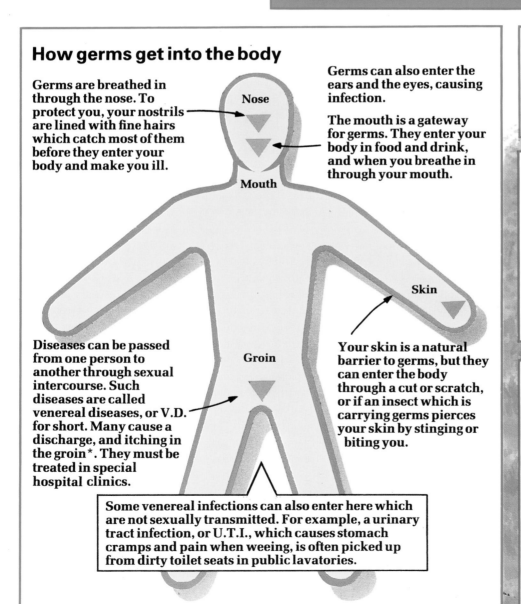

Germs are breathed in through the nose. To protect you, your nostrils are lined with fine hairs which catch most of them before they enter your body and make you ill.

**Nose**

**Mouth**

Germs can also enter the ears and the eyes, causing infection.

The mouth is a gateway for germs. They enter your body in food and drink, and when you breathe in through your mouth.

**Skin**

Your skin is a natural barrier to germs, but they can enter the body through a cut or scratch, or if an insect which is carrying germs pierces your skin by stinging or biting you.

**Groin**

Diseases can be passed from one person to another through sexual intercourse. Such diseases are called venereal diseases, or V.D. for short. Many cause a discharge, and itching in the groin*. They must be treated in special hospital clinics.

Some venereal infections can also enter here which are not sexually transmitted. For example, a urinary tract infection, or U.T.I., which causes stomach cramps and pain when weeing, is often picked up from dirty toilet seats in public lavatories.

## How infections spread

This picture shows some of the ways in which infections spread from one person to another.

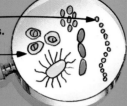

### Droplet method

When you have an infection such as 'flu, the virus lives in your nose and throat. It is passed to other people when you breathe out, cough or sneeze. The viruses are in drops of liquid in your breath. This is the droplet method of spreading infection.

### Contact

Some infections are spread by direct contact. A condition called herpes causes a sore, usually around the mouth or the groin. If someone touches it, or touches something the infected person has used – such as a towel – the virus causing herpes can burrow into their skin and the illness develops. This is the contact method of spreading infection.

*See pages 30-31 for a diagram of the sexual organs.

## Fungi

Mushrooms, toadstools and mould are all different types of fungi (singular fungus). Certain kinds of fungus can grow on the body too and cause infections.

Athlete's foot is caused by particles

Raw, flaky skin caused by athlete's foot.

called ringworm fungus which grow between the toes, making the skin flaky and crusty. These are picked up in places with damp floors such as swimming baths. Athlete's foot is treated using ointment or powder.

## Protozoa

Protozoa (singular protozoan) are another type of germs. They are tiny single-celled animals rather like bacteria. Most of them are completely harmless but some can cause disease.

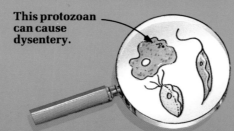

This protozoan can cause dysentery.

One kind of protozoan can live in the human intestine and cause a disease called dysentery, for which the symptoms are vomiting and acute diarrhoea. Dysentery is quite rare in most parts of the world.

## Worm infections

Infections are also caused by different types of worms. One of them is the hookworm, which lives in water and soil in some countries. People can be infected by them if they walk bare-

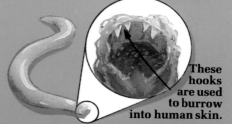

These hooks are used to burrow into human skin.

footed. The worms eggs, called larvae, burrow through the skin of feet and ankles and are carried through the blood system. There they develop into adult worms, which cause the illness.

## Water-borne infections

Water can carry infections, especially in places where there is no sewage system or clean water supply. A river, for example, might be used by a whole village as drinking water and as a place to wash. If people with an infection use the river as a toilet, germs are passed into the water where they live and develop. The infection is then passed to people using the river for other purposes.

Cholera is an example of a disease passed on by contaminated water. People can die from the terrible diarrhoea it causes.

This man has an infectious disease.

The water is contaminated by him and these people are in danger of catching the disease.

## What is an epidemic?

An epidemic is a large outbreak of one infectious disease. The most recent and serious examples are the outbreaks of a new bacterial infection called Legionnaires' disease, first diagnosed in 1976. It causes symptoms similar to 'flu, which is dangerous as the disease can kill if left untreated.

## How insects carry disease

Insects such as flies, fleas and mosquitos can infect people with germs picked up, for example, from animals. This is called the vector method of spreading disease.

### Flies

A fly can pick up germs in dirty places such as rubbish dumps. The germs stick to the fly's feet or hairy body. When

Sticky legs

the fly lands on some food, the germs are passed onto it and can infect the person who eats it.

### Fleas

Fleas feed on animals by sucking their blood. They also bite humans and can pass on disease from an infected animal.

About 300 years ago, millions of people died from the Plague, a disease carried by fleas living on rats.

### Mosquitos

Piercer

A type of mosquito which lives in hot, swampy countries carries protozoa germs (see above) which produce a disease called

malaria in people bitten by the mosquito.

9

# How your body fights illness

Your body is an amazing fighting machine designed to combat the germs and hazards in the world. It heals when you cut it and will fight most germs successfully.

The picture on the left is colour coded to show which main systems work together to prevent germs from making you ill. For example, the stomach is part of the alimentary canal which contains substances which destroy germs.* There are also lumps called lymph nodes, situated all over the body, which produce chemicals to kill germs.

Each system is described individually below. You can find out opposite how the same systems help to heal broken bones and cuts.

## 1  Alimentary canal

The alimentary canal is lined by mucous membrane which is wet and slippery. Its main function is to break down the food you eat into useful substances. It also protects you from illness because the juice in your stomach contains acids which kill many germs.

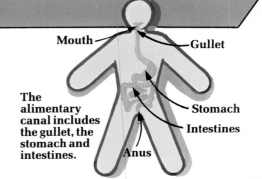

Mouth — Gullet

The alimentary canal includes the gullet, the stomach and intestines.

Stomach

Intestines

Anus

## 2  Warning systems

There is a complicated network of nerves inside you. Their job is to send messages to your brain which identifies sensations such as smell, pain, heat and noise. Without such a system, your body could be damaged without you realizing. The nervous system acts as a warning system about injury and illness.

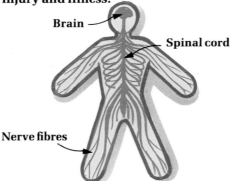

Brain

Spinal cord

Nerve fibres

### Nerve cells

Your nervous system is made up of nerve cells which vary greatly in shape and size. Most of them are situated in your brain and the top of your spinal cord. Attached to each cell are long fibres which reach all parts of your body. Some of the nerve-endings are just beneath your skin while others are attached to muscles and organs. There are lots of them in your hands, feet, and round your mouth.

### How nerves work

Each nerve fibre under your skin is called a receptor because it receives sensations. The nerves send messages in the form of pulses of electricity which reach your brain in a fraction of a second.

When you prick your finger on a pin, the receptor sends a lightning message to the nerve centres in your brain and spinal cord.

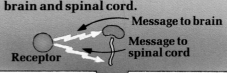

Message to brain

Message to spinal cord

Receptor

Your brain sends a message via the spinal cord telling your finger to move away from the pin. This is a reflex action.

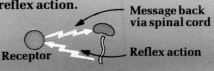

Message back via spinal cord

Reflex action

Receptor

Your brain searches your memory and sends back a message identifying the pin as the cause of pain.

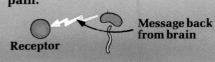

Receptor

Message back from brain

---

The alimentary canal is shown in gold.

The nervous system is shown in green.

The lymph nodes (see opposite page) are shown in blue.

The blood system is shown in red.

**10**

*The alimentary canal is part of the digestive system.*

Your blood contains special white blood cells called lymphocytes. When germs penetrate your blood system, lymphocytes produce chemicals called antibodies to fight them. The antibodies attach themselves to germs and either neutralize or destroy them.

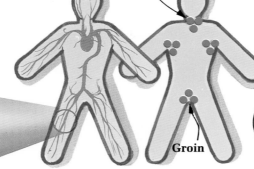

Lymph nodes

Groin

Antibodies

Germs

Lymphocytes are made in your bone marrow and in small swellings called lymph nodes which are all over your body, especially in your neck, armpits and groin. The main function of lymphocytes is to produce antibodies.

You produce antibodies in response to particular germs. The antibodies you produce against one kind of illness will not be effective against another.

## How bones heal

When you break a bone, a blood clot forms in much the same way as over a cut. Capillaries move in and supply blood to the damaged bone which it needs to start the healing process. Special cells called osteoblasts, which make bone, move into the area and reproduce quickly, knitting the broken ends of the bone together. This process takes from a few weeks to months depending on where and how the bone is broken.

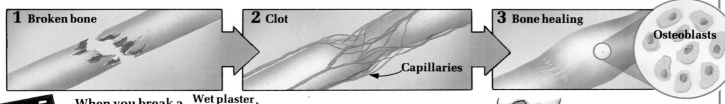

**1** Broken bone

**2** Clot

Capillaries

**3** Bone healing

Osteoblasts

X-ray

Break

When you break a bone, an X-ray is taken so that the doctor can see exactly where it is broken and how badly.*

Wet plaster bandage

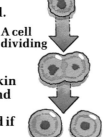

If you break an arm or a leg, the doctor will soak in water a bandage impregnated with plaster, then wrap it around the broken limb.

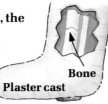

Bone

Plaster cast

The plaster hardens to form a tube in the shape of your arm or leg so that the broken bone is held together in the right position.

## Cell replacement

Your body is constantly manufacturing new cells to replace those that have died. A red blood cell, for instance, has an average life of only four months.

Food provides the basic nutrients needed to make new cells. The speed of this process varies. For example, new skin grows within a few days, while bones and organs take weeks to heal. Some cells, such as muscle cells, cannot be replaced if they die. This is why it is important to keep them in good working order through exercise.

A cell dividing

## How cuts heal

When you cut yourself, the blood round the cut clots, hardens and forms a scab. New tissue begins to grow underneath the scab, pulling the cut skin together. The scab gradually shrinks, then falls off when the new tissue has repaired the damaged skin.

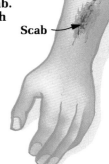

Graze

Scab

Deep cut

Suture

Knot

Sometimes if a cut is very deep, the doctor might stitch it up to help the skin knit together more quickly and stop the bleeding. This is done with a short, curved needle and special sterile thread called suture. The stitches are put in one at a time and individually knotted. This makes the stitch strong, and easy to remove. During an operation, dissolving stitches are sometimes put into the tissue below the skin, as well as ordinary ones in the skin itself.

## Getting better

The period when your body is recovering from illness or injury is called convalescence.

Convalescence is especially needed after a serious illness, or an accident which involves the loss of a lot of blood. This can put the body in a state of shock, which means that it stops functioning properly, and the healing process takes longer to begin.

*See page 24.

# Preventative medicine

Preventing illness is just as important as curing it. Doctors, medical scientists and health officers spend much of their time looking for ways of controlling and wiping out illness. This is called preventative medicine.

One of the most important aspects of preventative medicine is dealing effectively with sewage and rubbish and providing clean drinking water. Other aspects of preventative medicine include regular medical check-ups and immunization.

On these two pages you can find out how lots of people work to keep you healthy and what you can do to look after your own body.

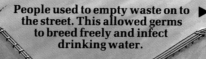
People used to empty waste on to the street. This allowed germs to breed freely and infect drinking water. ▶

Sewage works purify and dispose of toilet and kitchen waste.

## Public health

Health officers are appointed by the government to visit factories, shops and restaurants, checking that conditions are clean and the food is fresh and safe to eat. Spot checks are carried out and samples of food taken away to be analysed in a laboratory. These safeguards help to prevent outbreaks of food poisoning and other infections.

A health officer checking a restaurant.

## Check-ups

Check-ups are carried out in schools and clinics to look for early signs of illness. This is called screening and is an important part of preventative medicine because it allows doctors to spot and treat any illness before it develops. For example, cancer of the cervix* has been prevented in many women because of a test, called a smear test, which shows the cancer developing before it establishes itself in the body.

Illness can be prevented by having check-ups.

## Immunization

One of the most important parts of preventative medicine is immunization against disease. This is when the doctor gives you a vaccine, which is a small amount of substance which usually causes a disease. It makes your body produce antibodies to kill those particular germs. Should you later come in contact with that disease, your body will recognize it and produce the antibodies to kill it before you get ill. You are then said to be immune to that disease.

Soon after birth, you are given your first set of vaccines to protect against diseases such as polio, which can affect limb growth. After a few years you might be given a further dose, called a booster, to make sure you are still immune. Vaccines against some diseases, such as measles, last for life.

Your body reacts to vaccines in different ways, and they travel round the body at different rates, depending upon how they are given. You might be given an injection, be pricked by a puncher with lots of small sharp needles on it, or be given tablets, or drops on sugar lumps.

Vaccine on sugar lumps.

Tablets containing vaccine.

These sharp needles scratch your skin. The vaccine then enters your bloodstream.

*The pictures on pages 30-31 show where the cervix is.

# Developing immunity

All babies are born with some immunity to disease which is passed on from their mother through the placenta. This immunity lasts for about six months. When it wears off, babies can only become immune by suffering a disease, which produces antibodies naturally, or through vaccination.

Vaccines are prepared from chemicals called antigens, taken from animals and people who have suffered the disease. They are made from samples of blood collected from blood donors, for example. Vets collect similar samples from animals.

Antigens being taken from a horse.

Vaccines are also prepared from samples of the disease itself collected in the same way as antigens, or cultured in a laboratory. The sample is weakened using heat or chemicals so that it is just strong enough to make the body produce antibodies, but not the disease.

People can also become immune to a disease by being given ready-made antibodies extracted from other people which the body adopts as its own.

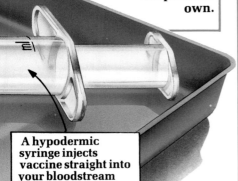

A hypodermic syringe injects vaccine straight into your bloodstream through a vein.

# Why you need to be immunized

Placenta

The baby receives food through the placenta. Rubella can cross it and infect the baby.

Sometimes there is a special reason to be immunized against particular illnesses.

It is very important, especially for girls, to be immunized against Rubella (German measles). Although it is not a serious disease, it can damage an unborn child if a pregnant woman catches it. Rubella is caused by a virus which damages the cells of the mother and baby. This affects the baby's growth and it can be born disabled.

Sometimes when you go abroad vaccines are needed against diseases not found in this country. This is both to protect you and to ensure that you do not bring any infection back home and start an epidemic. *

It is very important not to take animals from one country to another. They can carry infections too. One of the worst is rabies, for which there is no cure. People catch rabies by being bitten by infected animals.

# Keeping yourself healthy

There are several things you can do yourself to keep healthy, such as eating a balanced diet, taking lots of exercise and avoiding things which damage your body such as smoking. (Never inhale the fumes of substances such as glue. They can damage organs and even kill.)

### Vitamins

Vitamins are chemicals which your body needs to work efficiently but cannot make itself.

Fruit

### Carbohydrates

Carbohydrates provide energy which you need for any physical activity. Some energy is made into heat, maintaining your body temperature of 37°C (98.4°F).

Bread

### Water

Water makes up about 70% of your body weight. It is contained in most food. Without any food or water you would die within days.

Water

It is a good idea to exercise as much as possible to keep your body in good working order. Exercise helps to keep your heart pumping efficiently and keeps your muscles strong. It also increases your lung capacity so that more oxygen gets into your body, and it helps you to burn off excess food. One of the best exercises is swimming because it uses all parts of your body at once.

Different food contains different substances needed by your body. These are protein, vitamins, minerals, water, fat, carbohydrate and roughage. The chart below lists the main foods in a balanced diet, and how they help your body.

### Fats

Fats provide more energy than carbohydrates, and also vitamins, some of which you cannot get any other way.

Cheese

### Protein

Protein is broken down and becomes acids called amino acids which your cells use for growth, and to repair tissues.

Meat

### Fibre

Fibre adds bulk to your diet and helps your waste products to keep moving.

Beans
Bran

### Minerals

Minerals are used in the construction of body tissues.

Vegetables

As part of preventative medicine, doctors educate people about the effects on their bodies of smoking, alcohol and drugs. They encourage and help people to avoid these things or give them up.

*See page 9.

# Going to see the doctor

People usually go to the doctor if they have had an accident, or need advice, a check-up, medicine, or an immunization. If they are ill, the doctor will ask questions and examine their body to find out what is wrong. This is called making a diagnosis.

The doctor uses special equipment to examine a patient, such as a sphegnamanometer to measure their blood pressure (see opposite page). When a diagnosis has been made, the doctor decides how to treat the patient. If medicine is needed, the doctor writes a prescription, which is an authorization to the chemist to provide the medicine. Prescriptions ensure that dangerous medicines are controlled.

## What is the doctor's job?

Doctors have to have a thorough knowledge of a healthy body to recognize the symptoms of an illness.

It helps to be a good listener and sympathetic towards people because an accurate diagnosis depends partly on what the patient says.

There are thousands of different kinds of medicines available. The doctor has to choose the right one for the patient and make sure they have no allergies* to any medicine, such as penicillin.

Sometimes the doctor will send patients to a specialist for a second opinion, or to hospital for tests or an operation.

The doctor has to keep up-to-date with all the new medicines and techniques available to give the patient the best treatment possible.

## Making a diagnosis

The doctor fits together the answers to questions like a jigsaw puzzle to make a diagnosis. She starts by asking about the general health and past illnesses of the patient. This is called taking a case history and it helps the doctor to know if a patient is prone to any illnesses. Below you can find out how a doctor diagnoses appendicitis.

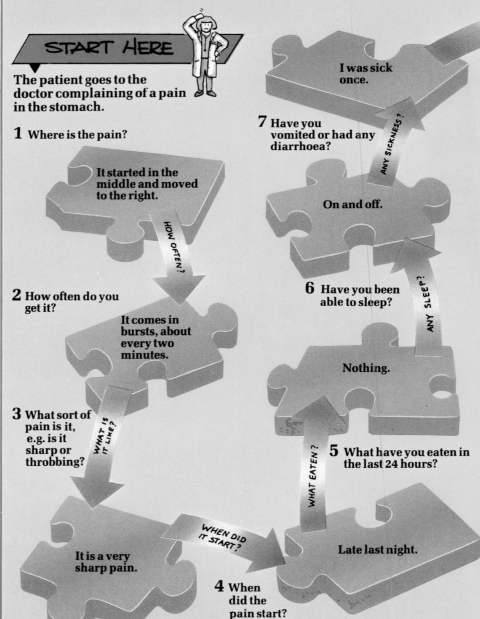

START HERE

The patient goes to the doctor complaining of a pain in the stomach.

**1** Where is the pain?

It started in the middle and moved to the right.

**2** How often do you get it?

HOW OFTEN?

It comes in bursts, about every two minutes.

**3** What sort of pain is it, e.g. is it sharp or throbbing?

WHAT IS IT LIKE?

It is a very sharp pain.

WHEN DID IT START?

**4** When did the pain start?

I was sick once.

**7** Have you vomited or had any diarrhoea?

ANY SICKNESS?

On and off.

ANY SLEEP?

**6** Have you been able to sleep?

Nothing.

WHAT EATEN?

**5** What have you eaten in the last 24 hours?

Late last night.

# A general examination

On the right you can find out what happens when the doctor checks a patient's body to find out if there is anything wrong. This is called a general examination.

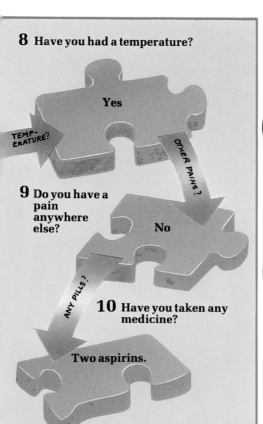

**8** Have you had a temperature?

Yes

TEMP-ERATURE?

OTHER PAINS?

**9** Do you have a pain anywhere else?

No

ANY PILLS?

**10** Have you taken any medicine?

Two aspirins.

Then the doctor will feel the patient's stomach all over. This hurts, but it is necessary for the doctor to find the tender part.

YOU HAVE APPENDICITIS

At this point the doctor might suspect that the patient has appendicitis and send them to hospital to have their appendix removed. You can find out about this operation on pages 20-21.

The doctor looks inside the eyes with a thin torch to make sure there are no infections or eyesight defects.

A different torch is used to check the ears to make sure there is not too much of a substance called wax which clogs up ears and affects the patient's hearing.

The doctor might look in the mouth to check the tonsils, and check there is no swelling in the patient's throat.

The doctor checks the patient's weight to make sure they are not too light or too heavy for their height.

The doctor takes the patient's pulse by putting three fingers over the main artery in the wrist. The pulse beats are then counted to see if the patient's blood is flowing at the normal rate.

The doctor listens to the patient's chest with a stethoscope. This is to make sure the heart and lungs are working properly.

The feet are checked in case there is athlete's foot or a fungus called a verucca which looks like a mole.

## Other equipment

The doctor also has lots of other equipment which might be used during an examination. For example, a blood pressure kit, syringes and needles for taking blood samples or giving immunizations (see page 12), sharp knives, a stick like a lollipop stick to take samples from the throat, and a hammer to tap the joint just below the knee-cap to check the patient's reflexes – if their knee jerks then all is well.

Syringe

Blood pressure kit

## Blood samples

Many infections can be detected in the blood. This is because invading germs use the bloodstream to move around the body. A small sample of blood taken from the arm is enough to show if germs are present. It can also show deficiencies in the blood, such as too few red blood cells which causes a condition called anaemia.

## Urine tests

Infections can be present in urine. Sometimes this can be seen by the doctor without sending a sample for analysis. There might be blood present, for example, or the urine might be a dark or pale colour, or have an abnormally thick consistency. A condition called diabetes is caused by too much sugar in the body which is detected in the urine.

## Blood pressure

Blood pressure is the force with which your heart pumps blood around your body. It is measured on a sphegnamanometer and recorded as two numbers written like a fraction. The top number, called the systolic, measures the pressure when the heart is pumping. The second number, called the diastolic, measures the pressure in between heart-beats when the heart is relaxed.

# Treating illnesses and injuries

Often your body will cope with an illness and you will get better without any help from medicines or doctors. Sometimes, however, you may need some medicine, or advice from a doctor on how to get better more quickly. The doctor might tell you to cut down on certain food such as chips, or do some special exercises, for instance. You can find out on these two pages about medicines and treatments. On pages 18-19, you can find out about alternative forms of treatment to those described here.

## About medicines

There are many different kinds of medicines, and they can be taken in different ways. Some are swallowed while others are injected or inhaled, or given in drops in the eyes and ears, or in tablets pushed up the back passage (rectum*).

Injection

Ear-drop

Tablet

Penicillin in mould, killing bacteria.

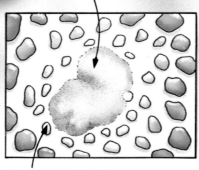

White neutralized bacterium

## How medicines work

Medicines called antibiotics work directly on bacteria, either preventing them from multiplying, or killing them completely. They are used to treat many illnesses from ear infections to pneumonia. ▶

Analgesics dissolve in your stomach and travel round your bloodstream.

Some medicines relieve ▲ symptoms of illnesses such as pain or fever, but do not actually kill the germs. They are called analgesics and include aspirin. Analgesics work in different ways; for instance by blocking the chemicals in your body which trigger pain fibres.

Some medicines are used to replace substances lacking in the body. Vitamin D, for instance, is needed for the proper growth of limbs. It can be given as medicine to people who lack it in their diet. ▼

This food contains vitamin D.

Overweight people often have high blood pressure.

A group of medicines called anti-hypertensives are used ◀ to bring down high blood pressure which is dangerous because it causes the heart to overwork.

Medicines are dangerous and are carefully controlled by doctors and chemists. Many can only be obtained if a doctor prescribes them with strict instructions as to when and how often

# DANGER

they should be taken. You should never touch any medicines without the knowledge of an adult. If they are mis-used they could make you very ill and even kill you.

All medicines act differently on the body. For this reason some have to be taken after a meal, and others on an empty stomach; some need to be mixed with water and others swallowed whole. It is always

important to follow the instructions on a medicine label very carefully as they are harmful unless correctly taken. If you do not complete a course of antibiotics, for instance, the bacteria may survive. They can then

build up an immunity to the substances in the antibiotic so that a dose in the future would be useless. A complete course of antibiotics kills all the bacteria.

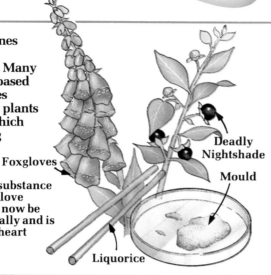

Most medicines are made in laboratories. Many of those are based on substances contained in plants and herbs which have healing properties.

**Foxgloves**

Digitalis is a substance found in foxglove leaves. It can now be made artificially and is used to treat heart disease.

**Deadly Nightshade**

**Mould**

**Liquorice**

Belladonna, or atropine, comes from a plant called deadly nightshade. An extraction from it is used to dry up saliva (spit) before an operation*.

Liquorice lines the stomach and is used to treat stomach ulcers caused by too much acid.

Penicillin is extracted from mould and it kills bacteria germs.

## Problems with medicines

Some medicines cause side-effects or allergic reactions. Common side-effects are vomiting, rashes, diarrhoea, sleepiness and indigestion. The doctor has to weigh the advantages against the disadvantages when prescribing medicines. If, for example, an illness is not serious and the medicine for it can cause side-effects just as unpleasant as the symptoms, then it is not worth taking the medicine. With more serious illnesses such as cancer, other medicine is given to control the side-effects of the medicines for the cancer.

## Physiotherapy

**Physiotherapist**

Physiotherapy consists of exercises given by specially trained people to anyone who cannot move properly. It is important because muscles start to waste away if they are not used. A physiotherapist uses massage, heat treatment, electrical treatment, and special exercises, sometimes carried out in a swimming pool.

After a stroke, for example, a physiotherapist will begin treatment quickly to prevent paralyzed muscles causing a leg or an arm to shorten, and to teach the patient to use other muscles to do the job of those that have failed.

## Special diet

Some illnesses are treated by a special diet. A stomach infection called gastro-entiritis causes vomiting and diarrhoea. A diet of water and clear soups helps the stomach to settle down again and the symptoms to disappear.

## Rest and exercise

Your body needs rest to recover from any illness and return to its full strength. After an injury such as a broken bone, however, exercise may be necessary even if it is painful. This is because muscles and bones become weak if they are not used. Inactivity can also stop your blood flowing as quickly as it should. This can cause blood clots to form which restrict the blood-flow.

## Occupational therapy

Occupational therapy means giving people activities, such as weaving baskets or painting, after they have had a serious illness or accident. This is to improve the concentration, or relieve the depression of those weakened by illness. Trained therapists also help someone learn a new trade or skill if they have been handicapped, and visit their home to see if any special aids need to be fitted, such as ramps for wheelchairs.

## Speech therapy

Speech therapy is used to help people who have speech defects or difficulties. After a stroke, for example, a speech therapist can help the patient recover speech through special voice exercises.

*See pages 20-21.

# Alternative medicine

On these two pages you can find out about some treatments which are not normally used by family doctors. Together, they are called complementary, or alternative, medicine and are often used alongside conventional treatments.

There are hundreds of different kinds of these treatments, some of which have been established for thousands of years. Some involve taking medicines, or remedies, which are made entirely of natural ingredients. One, called osteopathy, uses massage and manipulation of bones, joints and muscles. Another, called acupuncture, uses fine needles which are pushed into the skin at certain places. The theory of most forms of alternative treatment is based on the idea that the body should contain a fine balance of things to stay healthy. When ill, the whole person should be treated and not the symptoms of a particular illness as in conventional medicine. In China, the theory is expressed in symbols called yin and yang. Together they represent all the functions of the body and mind and stand for the perfect balance of positive and negative forces. When they are unbalanced, through eating the wrong food, for example, then you become ill. Many alternative treatments are based on the ideas of people who were conventional doctors but developed their own theories about how people should be treated. Now, many therapists are not doctors but are trained in one alternative treatment.

*Herbs are crushed to make medicine.*

*Osteopathy*

*Yin Yang symbol*

## Going to see a natural therapist

Natural therapists take a case history and make a diagnosis just like ordinary doctors. The procedure for doing this is slightly different though. For instance, a therapist might ask much more detailed questions about yourself and your past, some of which do not seem to have anything to do with your illness. They will also note the way you walk and talk, and whether you are shy or outgoing. This is because the therapist believes that you must be treated as a whole, not just your illness, and that each individual responds to a different kind of treatment.

*The therapist notes this man's slouch as well as his symptoms.*

## Acupuncture

Acupuncture is an ancient Oriental treatment based on the idea that all things contain a life force called Chi. Chi flows along invisible lines in the body called meridian lines. On these lines are hundreds of invisible points called pressure points. An acupuncturist acts on these points mainly by applying needles. They might also use finger pressure, heat, lasers or ultrasound. The treatment is not always in the same area as the illness. For example, someone with a kidney complaint might be given treatment in their ear by an acupuncturist.

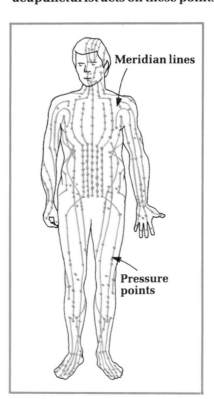

Meridian lines

Pressure points

An acupuncturist decides which parts of the body need to be treated and sticks fine needles into the pressure point areas. Surprisingly, this does not hurt at all because the

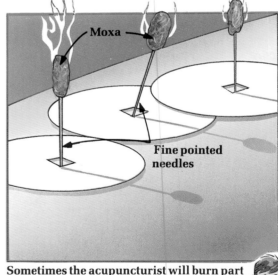

Moxa

Fine pointed needles

Sometimes the acupuncturist will burn part of a dried mugwort plant called moxa on the ends of the needles. This generates soothing heat down the needles and into your body and is called moxibustion.

acupuncturist knows exactly where and how to stick in the needles. This requires much experience and training and you should never try it yourself.

## Homeopathy

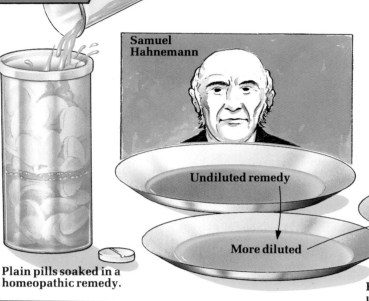

Homeopathic medicine is based on the principle that symptoms of illness are caused by the body's fight against it and not by the illness itself. This is generally known as the "like cures like" theory because, in healthy people, homeopathic medicine actually causes the symptoms you are trying to treat.

Plain pills soaked in a homeopathic remedy.

Samuel Hahnemann

Undiluted remedy

More diluted

More diluted

Remedy ready for use, extremely diluted.

Homeopathic medicine was founded about 200 years ago by a German doctor called Samuel Hahnemann. Experimenting with alternative remedies was not new, but Hahnemann discovered that the remedies worked much better if they were extremely diluted – sometimes so that hardly a drop of the medicine remained. Many conventional doctors found this hard to accept and it was a long time before homeopathy was established.

## Osteopathy

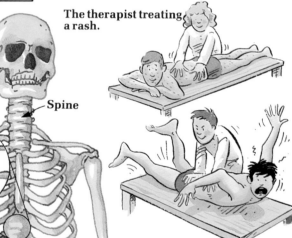

Osteopathy is concerned with the manipulation of joints, particularly in the region of the spine. It was founded by a doctor called Andrew Taylor Still over a hundred years ago. It is based on the idea that we become ill if any part of the spine is out of place. The theory developed because the spine and spinal cord are central to the body's structure and the nervous system *

Spine

Spinal cord

The therapist treating a rash.

The high velocity thrust.

Many people go to an osteopath if they have "ricked" their back, and they are treated by a simple manipulation of the spine. But the osteopath's field is wider and they can treat rashes, stomach upsets and headaches, for example, by manipulation of the joints.

The actual manipulation can be quite vigorous; one technique is called "the high velocity thrust". Others are very gentle, coaxing the tissues of the patient to respond. The osteopath decides on a different technique for different patients.

## Psychological therapies

Many alternative treatments are based on the idea that the mind can control illness; that it is caused by a depressed or anxious mental state and can be cured by an effort of will. These treatments are called psychological therapies and are close to the branch of medicine called psychiatry.

Many people do yoga to help them relax. They often find it increases their general mental and physical health and relieves aches and pains.

Sigmund Freud developed psychoanalysis about a hundred years ago. This involves talking to a patient in a special way to draw out of them things that are troubling them, making them depressed and ill. The patient often experiences a sense of release through this and finds that their health improves.

Many of Freud's ideas have now been changed or rejected altogether, but he is the father of the now extensive branch of psychological medicine.

## Hypnotherapy

It has been known for thousands of years that people can be put into a trance, rather like walking in your sleep. This is called hypnotism and is a psychological therapy. The idea behind hypnotherapy is that the patient relaxes and answers truthfully all the questions asked by the therapist. This allows a diagnosis to be made. Further sessions are used to reduce pain, or to enable a patient to stop worrying, helping the symptoms of an illness go away.

Hypnotism is most effective when the patient's illness is related to stress, or in helping people to give up cigarettes or alcohol.

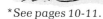

*See pages 10-11.

# Operations

Operations range from heart transplants, which take hours, to having a wart removed, which only takes seconds.

All operations are part of the branch of medicine called surgery. They are usually carried out in hospitals by specially trained doctors called surgeons in a room called an operating theatre. This is kept free of germs and has all the equipment to deal with major operations. On these two pages you can find out what happens during an operation to remove the appendix, called an appendicectomy.

An operating theatre is called a theatre because it used to be built as one. Students used to watch the operations in tiered seats all around. Now they watch them on special video screens.

## Reasons for operating

Most operations are straightforward and many can be done in less than half an hour. For example, a surgeon might do several tonsil operations (tonsillectomies) a day. Other operations are exploratory; the surgeon opens someone up to find out what is wrong with them.

Emergency operations are carried out, for example, after road accidents, or because of infections such as appendicitis which must be dealt with immediately.

## Preparing for an operation

Although the idea of an operation may be frightening, techniques and equipment are so sophisticated that there is no need to feel nervous. Follow the steps on the right to find out what happens during an appendicectomy.

Time-elapse clock to measure how long the patient is on a machine.

Clock

Surgeon

## Who is in the operating theatre?

For a minor operation, it is only necessary to have the surgeon and one nurse present, and an anaesthetist who monitors the patient's response to the anaesthetic and regulates their breathing. The nurse is there to pass instruments to the surgeon and generally assist at the operation. At a major operation there will be a surgeon and a junior surgeon and possibly a student as well as two nurses, the anaesthetist and some technicians to help operate some of the sophisticated equipment in the operating theatre. The surgeon's team is called a firm.

There is a large selection of cutting instruments; some small and thin for delicate surgery and others large and strong for cutting through bone, for example.

Everyone in the firm wears completely sterile clothes; a gown, rubber boots, gloves, a cap, and a mask over their mouths. This is to prevent the spread of germs. All the instruments used are also sterilized.

There are sterile containers where the surgeon puts samples that are sent to the laboratory for analysis.

A range of cotton swabs are used to wipe up blood from the patient, and needles and suture for sewing up the wounds.

**1** The patient is not given anything to eat or drink for several hours before the operation. It can be dangerous if there is food in his stomach while he is unconscious (anaesthetised). If he is sick during the operation, any food could make him choke.

**2** Never be afraid to ask a doctor or nurse any questions if you are having an operation.

A hospital doctor sees him to make sure he is ready. This doctor will probably be present at the operation. Sometimes the surgeon who will operate will come and see him too to explain what is going to happen.

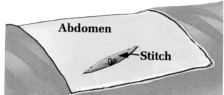

Special equipment, such as an electric knife which makes a clean bloodless cut, are connected overhead. This is to keep the operating theatre free of cables which might cause an accident.

Adjustable lights which do not cast shadows.

The temperature in the operating theatre is kept even so that any change in the patient's temperature is noticed immediately.

X-rays of the patient are pinned here.

Nurses

Anaesthetist

Patient

Anaesthetic supply

The Latin suffix -ectomy means "cutting out". An appendicectomy means "cutting out the appendix".

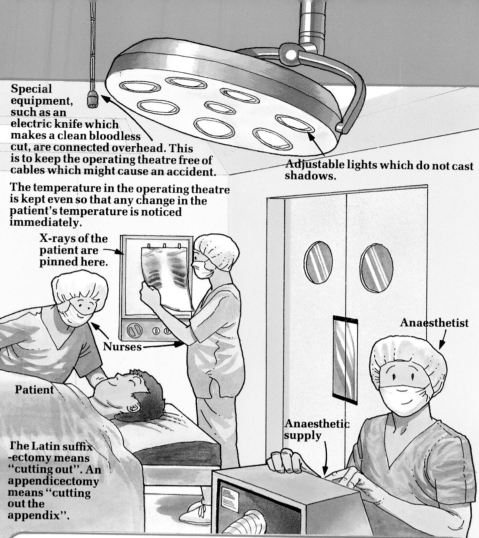

## The operation

The surgeon makes a cut about 8cm (3in) long in the skin on the right hand side of the abdomen using a very sharp knife called a scalpel.

Abdomen

Stitch

The skin and tissue underneath it opens up and the surgeon can then see the appendix attached to the end of the small intestine.* He puts a stitch at the top of the appendix and pulls it tight to cut off the blood supply, then slices off the appendix with another sharp knife.

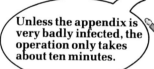

Suture

Appendix

The surgeon then sews the tissue together using dissolving suture. Finally the skin is sewn up with ordinary suture. The appendix is put in a sterile container and sent to the laboratory for analysis. This is necessary as doctors are still unsure what causes appendicitis.

Unless the appendix is very badly infected, the operation only takes about ten minutes.

The operation is now complete. The anaesthetist administers a drug which reverses the anaesthetic and the patient wakes up after a few minutes in the recovery room.

## After the operation

The patient might feel a bit sick when he wakes up, which is just the after-effects of the anaesthetic. He might feel thirsty too because the pre-med dries out the mouth. If he tries to move too much immediately, the area round the stomach will feel stiff and sore. The next day, however, he will have to get up and start using his muscles again so that they do not stiffen up.

Recovery room

### In the past

Only just over a hundred years ago, operations were carried out with no anaesthetic at all. Conditions were very unhygienic and many patients died because of germs picked up on the operating table. In 1865, a doctor called Joseph Lister used a spray disinfectant called carbolic during operations to kill the germs in the air. This was the basis of modern germ-free surgery.

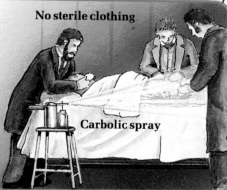

No sterile clothing

Carbolic spray

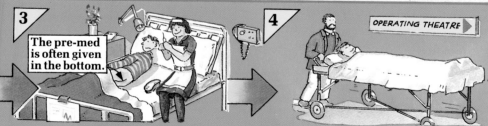

**3** The pre-med is often given in the bottom.

A nurse will give the patient an injection, or a syrup, to make him drowsy and relaxed and to dry up excess fluids in the mouth. This is called a pre-med.

**4** OPERATING THEATRE ▶

The patient is dressed in a loose gown and wheeled to the operating theatre on a trolley. The anaesthetic, usually administered in the form of an injection, is given before the patient goes into theatre.

*See page 7.

# How a hospital works

A hospital is run by a team of doctors, nurses, administrators, technicians, porters, cleaners, cooks, laundry workers and many more. It is a complicated organization of units, each of which specializes in one kind of illness or treatment. There are also departments in a hospital for physiotherapy and occupational therapy, and laboratories where scientists analyse samples taken from patients.

A team of administrators is in charge of the smooth-running of the whole hospital, while doctors and nurses are in charge of all the patients. The senior hospital doctors are specialists in one type of illness or area of the body. A paediatrician, for example is a specialist in children's illnesses. On these two pages you can find out about the different departments of a hospital.

## Reasons for going to hospital

Some people only visit the hospital when they need treatment or the use of special equipment. They go to a special section of the hospital called out-patients.

Usually about half the patients in hospital need an operation. They are called surgical patients.

Some people visit special clinics in the hospital. Pregnant women, for example, visit the ante-natal clinic where they are given a check-up.

Exploratory operations and other tests are done in hospital. One of these is a lumbar puncture in which spinal fluid is drained from the spine through a long needle to test it for diseases such as meningitis.

Others go when they have had an accident and need emergency treatment. They are taken to the accident-emergency unit, sometimes by ambulance.

## Units in a hospital

There are lots of different units in a hospital. Each has a special name and a specialist doctor in charge called a consultant. You can find out below what the units are called and what goes on in them.

|  |  |
|------|-------------|
| **Geriatrics** | This unit specializes in the care of old people. |
| **Haematology** | Blood disorders are treated here. |
| **Intensive care** | This unit looks after the seriously ill. |
| **ENT** | ENT stands for Ear, Nose and Throat and specializes in those parts of the body. |
| **Maternity** | Where babies are born. |
| **Cardiology** | This unit deals with heart disorders. |
| **Radiography** | Where X-rays are taken, and X-ray treatment is given (see page 24). |
| **Renal** | Kidney diseases are treated here. |
| **Physiotherapy** | This is where people improve mobility after an illness or accident. |
| **Psychiatry** | This unit deals with mental illness. |
| **Outpatients** | Where people go who do not have to stay in the hospital to be treated. |
| **Paediatrics** | Children's diseases are treated here. |
| **Blood bank** | Blood from donors is stored here for those who need transfusions. |
| **Orthopaedics** | This unit specializes in bone disorders. |
| **Pharmacy** | The medicines taken by the patients are prepared here. |
| **Dermatology** | Skin diseases are treated here. |
| **Operating theatres** | This is where the operations are performed. |

## Wards

Each hospital unit is divided into wards, which are rooms containing two rows of beds. Some wards hold one or two patients, while others hold up to fifty at a time.

Curtains

Each bed in a ward has curtains that are pulled round it if the patient needs some privacy.

There is a room in each ward where the nurses keep supplies such as bed-pans (which are used by patients unable to walk to the toilet), and medicines.

Each ward is run by a senior nurse called a sister who organizes the duties of the junior nurses and is responsible for giving the treatments prescribed by the doctor.

## Hospital for the healthy

Hospitals do not just look after ill people. For example, there is usually a maternity section where babies are born. This is kept apart from other units so that new babies do not come into contact with infectious illnesses.

Births are supervized in hospital by midwives and

doctors, called obstetricians, in case anything goes wrong. Premature babies (those born early) are put in machines called incubators which regulate the air temperature, acting a bit like the mother's womb, until the baby can manage on its own.

## Out-patients

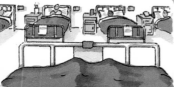

Often out-patients go to see specialists who are based in the hospital and are in charge of a unit there.

The specialist examines and treats them in the same way as a family doctor does, but if they need to be admitted to the hospital, the specialist can arrange it immediately.

Out-patients visit hospital to use special equipment. People with heart trouble, for example, can be connected to a machine which prints out their heartbeat as a graph, helping the doctor detect any defects. This test is called an electro-cardiograph, or E.C.G.

E.C.G. print-out

People visit the physiotherapy unit as out-patients for check-ups on their progress. Sometimes they are sent after treatment for a broken bone at the accident-emergency unit. The therapist will give them a walking aid and teach them how to use it.

## Running the hospital

The hospital administrators are in charge of all these things. They control the hospital's money and decide what to spend it on after discussion with the medical staff. They are also in charge of paying the salaries of the people employed by the hospital.

Hospitals are extremely expensive to run. They also have to run smoothly and efficiently and need a constant supply of equipment.

The administrators also make sure the hospital has, for example, enough back-up electricity generators to deal with emergencies such as power cuts. Many life-saving machines depend on electricity.

# Technology and medicine

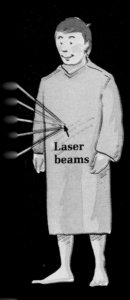

Laser beams

Many of the latest advances in medicine use technology developed for non-medical purposes. Lasers, for example, are used in industry for drilling, cutting, welding and engraving. They are also used in surgery to make bloodless cuts and perform delicate operations. On these two pages you can find out about some of the technology which has revolutionized medicine over the last hundred years.

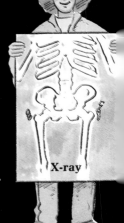

X-ray

## Looking inside the body

To make an accurate diagnosis of some illnesses without surgery it is essential to be able to see and photograph inside the body. There are now many techniques for doing this, some of which are also used to treat any abnormalities found.

Pictures of the inside of the body were first taken using X-rays in 1895. These enabled doctors to see if bones were broken or growths developing.

### About X-rays

X-rays are part of the "electromagnetic spectrum", which includes light, radio waves and microwaves. These "waves" travel at the same speed, but their wavelengths are different, giving them different properties. Unlike light waves, X-rays can travel through the flesh of the body, but are absorbed by bone, in particular the calcium in them. When X-rays are directed at the body a shadow of the bones appears on a

X-ray machine

Radiologist

Photographic plate

Protective lead * apron

photographic plate behind it. If exposed for too long, X-rays destroy the body's tissue. With care, they can be used to destroy diseased tissue in people suffering from cancer. This is called radiotherapy.

People who specialize in X-ray medicine are called radiologists. They wear protective clothing because continual exposure to X-rays is dangerous.

## Lasers inside the body

Lasers are often used in conjunction with an endoscope – a tube about as thick as a finger which is pushed into the patient's body, often down their throat. Endoscopes are used to see and remove things, such as growths, inside the body. They consist of glass fibre (fibre optic) cables which are made of hair-like strands of glass, through which ordinary light and laser light can be passed. Each cable has a different function. One, for example,

is used to light the body, and another to suck out samples for analysis.

A doctor guides the endoscope at one end, watching its progress through a magnifying glass. The inside of the body is reflected onto the glass from the light-reflecting fibre optic cables. A pincer at the other end grasps the growth. The doctor can then send a laser beam down one cable to destroy the growth and seal, or cauterize, the wound.

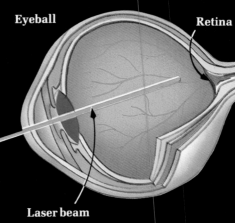

Eyeball

Retina

Laser beam

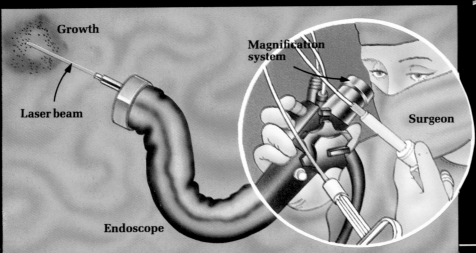

Growth

Laser beam

Magnification system

Surgeon

Endoscope

Lasers are also used in eye surgery, which is a particularly delicate organ to work on. The intense laser light beam is directed straight through the eyeball, like ordinary light, to the part which needs surgery. If the patient has, for example, a detached retina, the laser welds the retina back in place with a tiny heat scar.

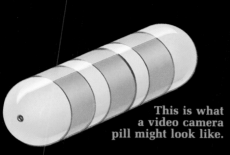

This is what a video camera pill might look like.

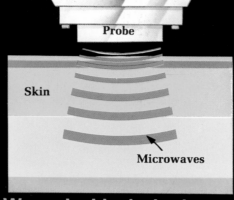

Probe

Skin

Microwaves

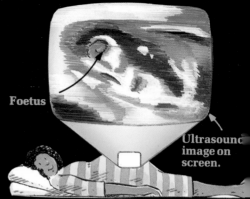

Foetus

Ultrasound image on screen.

Pregnant woman

## Video cameras

One of the new techniques being developed at the moment is a video camera which looks exactly like a pill and can be swallowed like one. It travels through a patient's body, transmitting pictures and information on the temperature and acidity of the patient's body to the doctor. This is done through a radio transmitter inside it.

## Waves inside the body

A new process using microwaves detects defects in tissue through a probe inserted into the body. At the moment, the microwaves only penetrate 4mm (⅛in) into the body, but a more powerful probe is being developed.

Ultrasound is a technique which uses sound waves to detect, for example, that an unborn child (foetus) is growing normally. It is used in place of X-rays on pregnant women, as doctors believe it is safer for the foetus.

## New operations

Sophisticated operations, such as organ transplants, depend on machines that have been developed to imitate one or several of the body's functions. They also depend on equipment such as an electric knife which makes clean bloodless cuts.

A transplant operation means removing a diseased organ from a patient and replacing it with a healthy one, usually taken from someone who has recently died from some other cause. Kidney, liver, heart, lung and cornea transplants have so far been performed.

The main danger of a transplant operation is the possibility of the patient's body rejecting the new organ in the same way as the body reacts against invading germs. Medicines are given to supress the immune system so that the patient does not form antibodies to fight the organ. This makes the patient very vulnerable to other infections until the organ is accepted.

## The heart-lung machine

This is a heart-lung machine to which a patient is connected during open heart surgery (which means the heart is opened up). Blood from the main arteries and veins is diverted through the machine while the surgeon works on the heart. The machine imitates the heart and lungs by pumping the blood round, supplying it with oxygen and removing carbon dioxide.

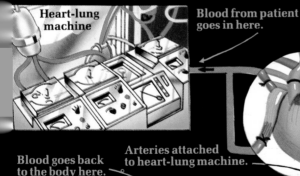

Heart-lung machine

Blood from patient goes in here.

New heart

Blood goes back to the body here.

Arteries attached to heart-lung machine.

## Microsurgery

Microsurgery is performed with the aid of a microscope. It is used for delicate operations which involve joining tiny blood vessels and nerves after an accident, or after they have been cut by the surgeon to reach another part of the body. It is often used for operations on the eye, and during organ transplants. It is essential in brain surgery (neurosurgery), where the centres which control all the body's functions are closely packed together and the surgeon has to see exactly where he is working.

Microsurgery has also made it possible to re-join limbs that are accidentally severed. In some cases, surgeons can sew the limb back on, re-connecting all the nerves, muscles, ligaments, tendons and blood vessels, so that, with physiotherapy, the limb works almost as efficiently as before.

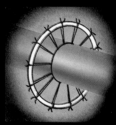

Using a microscope to see, a surgeon suspends a metal ring round a small vein to hold the suture in place while the ends are being joined.

## Breakthroughs in the laboratory

Many medical advances are chemical ones, made "behind the scenes" in the laboratory by scientists who have developed amazing new tests and medicines. For example, all newly born babies

A modern laboratory

are tested for thyroid deficiency – a condition which stunts a child's growth and leaves them with irreperable brain damage. Through a simple test, the condition can now be detected in time to treat the affected children, who then develop completely normally.

# Health and the environment

Peoples' health depends on what job they have, where they live and what kind of habits they have. A forester, for instance, who lives in the country and neither smokes nor drinks is more likely to be healthy than a factory worker who lives in a smoky city and drinks beer

every night. All the things around you, natural or man-made, are your environment. On these two pages, you can find out how environment affects the health of individuals and whole populations.

## Health at work

Some jobs involve working in places which have a high level of dust or toxic fumes which pollute the air. Mines, factories, chemical plants, laboratories and X-ray units in hospitals are all examples of working environments which are potentially dangerous to health. Coal dust in mines can cause pneumoconiosis, silica dust in quarries causes silicosis, and asbestos dust causes asbestosis. These are all diseases of the lung which develop over a number of years. Safety precautions are strict in working places at risk. In some factories workers wear special filter masks to avoid breathing in dust and fumes.

This sign denotes a radioactive area.

Protective clothing in a nuclear power plant.

Overshoes containing lead.

Welder

Fireman

Miner

Chemical worker.

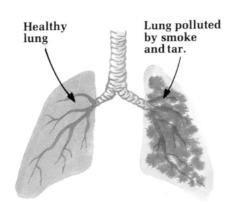

Healthy lung

Lung polluted by smoke and tar.

In nuclear power stations where they are dealing with radioactive materials, the workers have to wear full protective clothing – even lead overshoes in case the floor is radioactive. These safety precautions, however, cannot eliminate the risks completely.

## Man's effect on the environment

Every country in the world is affected by the problem of pollution. Poisonous substances escape from cars, factories and chemical plants. Pollution does not disappear, it goes into the air and circulates there, sometimes travelling hundreds of miles. It can change the environment and even affect the chemical composition of the atmosphere. The health of whole populations could be at risk if pollution increases.

To keep pollution under control, measures have been introduced such as making cities smokeless zones, introducing lead-free petrol, and fitting exhaust filters on cars. There is still the long-term problem of how to dispose of the enormous quantities of waste from chemical plants, some of which is radioactive, and how to prevent disasters such as spillages from oil tankers. These things have a direct effect on the health of those who live nearby, including plants and animals.

Sea-bird trapped in an oil-slick.

## Passive smoking

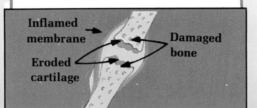

Smoking is a form of pollution and a very dangerous habit, causing diseases such as bronchitis and lung cancer. Smokers are not the only ones at risk. If a non-smoker works in a room full of smokers, they can contract the same diseases (although it is less likely). This is called passive smoking.

## Living conditions

Poor sanitation*, dampness and overcrowded living conditions in the home contribute to the development of illness. A disease called tuberculosis (TB), which is a bacterial infection (usually of the lungs), is easily spread in overcrowded communities. Rheumatism, a condition which stiffens joints, is more likely to affect people who live in damp houses, or near the sea where there is dampness in the air.

The picture below shows a rheumatic knee-joint.

Inflamed membrane

Damaged bone

Eroded cartilage

## The World Health Organization

The World Health Organization (WHO), keep a constant up-to-date supply of information on the state of health of people from every country. It gives specialist advice to governments of countries that have a health problem (such as how to control the spread of disease after a natural disaster). It also campaigns to control infections such as malaria, through immunization and drainage of swamps where disease-carrying mosquitos live.

The WHO also organizes educational programs to teach people about nutrition, sanitation and immunization – three of the most important factors in disease control.

## Climate

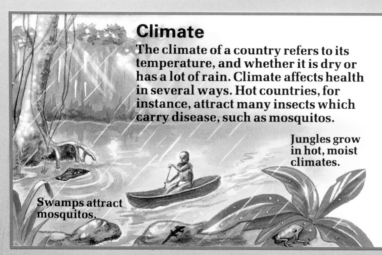

Swamps attract mosquitos.

The climate of a country refers to its temperature, and whether it is dry or has a lot of rain. Climate affects health in several ways. Hot countries, for instance, attract many insects which carry disease, such as mosquitos.

Jungles grow in hot, moist climates.

Most areas of the world have variable climates. Countries very far north or south of the equator, however, have long summers or winters and this can affect health. In parts of Northern Russia, for instance, there is so little daylight during the winter that the children need to be exposed to ultra-violet light from a machine every day. This is to provide the vitamins which are usually made by the skin after contact with the sun, and which are essential for bone growth.

## Diet

The food people eat affects their health. A poor diet causes deficiency diseases such as rickets which stunts the growth of bones. It deprives the body of the basic nutrients it needs to make antibodies to fight germs. This leads to low resistance to infections which are mild in people with a good diet. In some countries, for example, measles is a serious disease, killing many children who are malnourished.
In many countries, there is no shortage of food, but people become ill through eating "junk food" such as cakes, chips and fizzy drinks. This food is not nutritious and tends to make you overweight which is also unhealthy. People who eat too much, drink too much alcohol and smoke are more likely to develop heart disease.
In countries where the diet is basic but nutritional, people tend not to develop illnesses such as appendicitis and stomach ulcers.

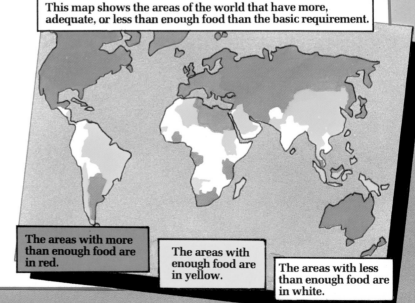

This map shows the areas of the world that have more, adequate, or less than enough food than the basic requirement.

The areas with more than enough food are in red.

The areas with enough food are in yellow.

The areas with less than enough food are in white.

*See pages 12-13.

# First aid

First aid means the first help given to someone if they are ill or have an accident. This ranges from giving them "the kiss of life" (artificial respiration), to putting a plaster over a cut.

Here, you can find out how to give some basic first aid, such as putting on a bandage, and how to deal with an emergency. A doctor should be consulted if an injury looks serious.

This picture shows useful things to have in a family medicine chest.

Scissors

Safety pins

Sticky plasters (air-strip so that the air can get to a cut through the holes).

Antiseptic ointment

Bandage

Needle

## DANGER
All medicines are dangerous. Never play with medicines and never take any medicine without asking an adult first.

## Splinters

A splinter is a tiny sliver of wood that gets wedged into the skin, usually your hand. Unless it is very tiny, it is best to remove it in case it is dirty and causes infection.

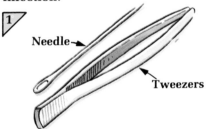

Needle

Tweezers

Remove a splinter using a needle and a pair of tweezers. Clean them with antiseptic liquid before use.

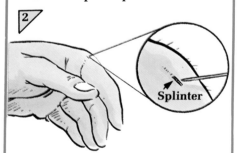

Splinter

Use the point of the needle to work free one end of the splinter without piercing the skin if possible.

Using tweezers, gently pull out the splinter and then wash the area with antiseptic liquid (or dab on some antiseptic ointment).

## Cuts

These steps show how to deal with a bleeding cut. If the cut is deep it should be seen by a doctor as it might need stitches.

Press firmly on the cut for three to five minutes using your hand, cotton wool, tissue, or a towel. This is to stop the bleeding.

Wash the cut gently using cotton wool and warm water, then dry it using a clean towel or tissue.

Put a piece of air-strip sticky plaster over the cut for a few days to keep it germ-free. Take the plaster off at night and replace it with a clean one in the morning. This allows air to reach the cut which helps it heal quickly.

## Using a bandage

If a cut is very dirty, or covers a large area, it is best to wash it carefully then put a bandage on it with a lint dressing. The steps below show you how to bandage an arm. You can use the same procedure for a leg cut.

Clean the wound with warm soapy water and cover it with gauze, or a piece of lint, smooth side down.

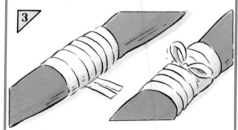

Make sure the arm is slightly bent. Take the bandage and wrap it round the arm firmly but not tightly. Cover the area 15cm (6in) above and below the cut.

Cut about 20cm (8in) down the centre of the free end of the bandage. Tie the cut ends together in a bow over the cut area.

Holes to allow air to the cut.

28

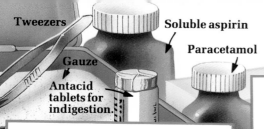

Tweezers

Soluble aspirin

Paracetamol

Lint

Gauze

Antacid tablets for indigestion.

Nose drops for stuffed up noses.

## Burns

Minor burns, which affect only the top layer of skin, heal very quickly although they can be very painful when they happen. If small blisters appear on a burn, they should not be burst.

Run the burnt area under the cold tap to cool it and help prevent blisters forming.

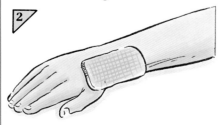

Cover it with something clean and dry, such as a tissue or a towel.

Superficial burn     Deep burn

If the burn is small with little blisters, keep it covered and dry for a few hours. See your doctor if it covers a large area or is deep and covered with dead skin.

## Bruises

The "black and blue" colours of a bruise are caused by blood gathering under the skin which comes from tiny blood vessels which burst when you knock them hard.

Most bruises have to be left to heal up by themselves. They will hurt for a few days so it is best to avoid situations when they might be knocked.

## Fainting

Fainting is caused by a lack of oxygen to the brain which makes you fall over. This is the body's way of getting the head down so that blood can travel back to the brain easily. It should only last for a minute or two. It is usually caused by hot weather, tiredness, lack of food, or standing still for too long.

If someone feels faint, sit them on a chair, put their head between their legs and fan the back of their neck until the feeling passes. It helps if they then sip a glass of water.

If someone actually faints, turn them on their side and make sure they can breathe properly. Loosen any tight collars and buttons round the neck. The picture above shows the exact position to put someone in who is unconscious – it is called the recovery position.

## At an accident

Do not move someone who has had an accident and cannot move themselves as they might have broken a bone. Make sure they can breathe properly, try to stop heavy bleeding by applying pressure to the area, and get help quickly if the person is unconscious or in a lot of pain. Especially never move anyone who has hurt their back.

## Artificial respiration

Artificial respiration means blowing into the lungs of someone who has stopped breathing, to start them working again. This should never be practised on people breathing normally.

Clear the patient's mouth of any objects such as chewing gum, false teeth, vomit or blood. Tilt their head back with the chin pushed forward. This is to clear the airways. Put your hand under the chin, open the mouth, and pinch the nostrils firmly together.

Take a deep breath and completely cover the patient's mouth with your own. Blow deeply into the lungs and repeat quickly four times to fill up the lungs with air.

Wait for the chest to fall. If the patient does not start breathing, repeat artificial respiration until they do or until help arrives.

You should always tell an adult or a doctor if someone hurts themselves badly. In serious cases, these are the three most important things to do until help arrives: make sure the patient can breathe easily, stop heavy bleeding and check that the person is conscious.

## Sprains and twists

A sprained ankle means that the ligaments which hold the bones together have been overstretched. This can happen quite easily. It usually causes the ankle to swell up and will be painful for a few days. All painful sprains should be seen by a doctor in case the bone is broken as well.

# Atlas of the body

When people study medicine, the first subject they learn is the structure of the human body. This is called anatomy. The pictures below show the main bones, organs and external features of a female and a male human body. You can use these as a reference guide as you read through the book.

## 2 Inside the body

In the pictures below, the male and female body show organs that are common to both, such as the heart, liver and lungs. They also show two of the body's systems – the blood system and nervous system. The female's sexual organs are the only difference between the bodies – they are labelled with an asterisk (*) to distinguish them.

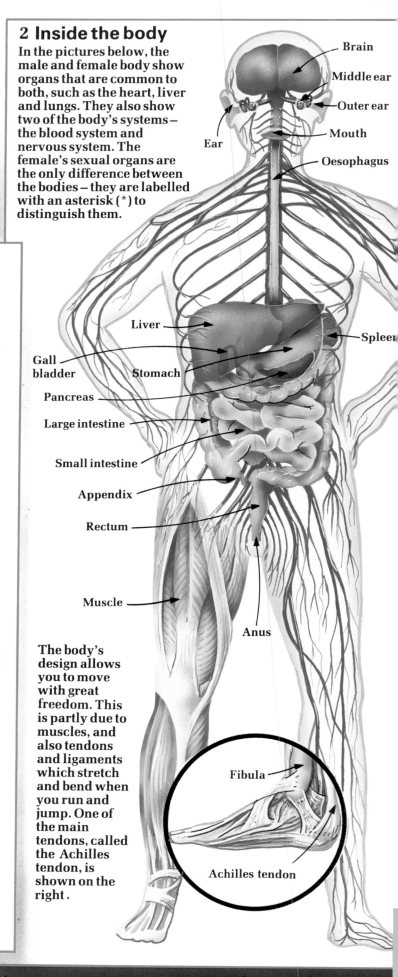

Brain
Middle ear
Outer ear
Ear
Mouth
Oesophagus
Liver
Spleen
Gall bladder
Stomach
Pancreas
Large intestine
Small intestine
Appendix
Rectum
Muscle
Anus

The body's design allows you to move with great freedom. This is partly due to muscles, and also tendons and ligaments which stretch and bend when you run and jump. One of the main tendons, called the Achilles tendon, is shown on the right.

Fibula
Achilles tendon

## 1 Outside the body

The pictures below show the external features of a male and female body. The main differences between them are in the sexual organs. Other external differences are that a woman has breasts and wider hips. A man has slightly broader shoulders, a less well-defined waist, and hairier skin, especially on his face.

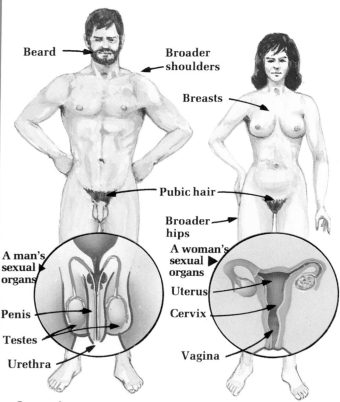

Beard
Broader shoulders
Breasts
Pubic hair
Broader hips
A man's sexual organs
A woman's sexual organs
Uterus
Penis
Cervix
Testes
Urethra
Vagina

### Sexual organs

A woman's sexual organs are inside the body while a man's are on the outside. The big picture on the right shows where the woman's sexual organs are positioned – they are labelled with an asterisk (*).

Men are usually stronger than women because their muscles are more developed. Women, however, often live longer than men and are more resistant to diseases such as heart disease.

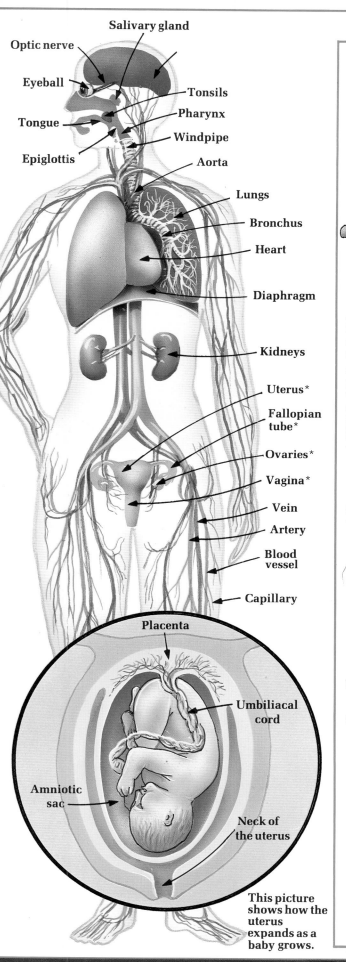

Optic nerve
Salivary gland
Eyeball
Tonsils
Tongue
Pharynx
Epiglottis
Windpipe
Aorta
Lungs
Bronchus
Heart
Diaphragm
Kidneys
Uterus*
Fallopian tube*
Ovaries*
Vagina*
Vein
Artery
Blood vessel
Capillary

Placenta
Umbiliacal cord
Amniotic sac
Neck of the uterus

This picture shows how the uterus expands as a baby grows.

## 3 The skeleton

The pictures below show the main bones in the human body. The male body is turned round to show the back view of the skeleton.

### How bones fit together

Bones fit together to make joints which allow you to move and bend. There are three main kinds of joints which are shown in the pictures below.

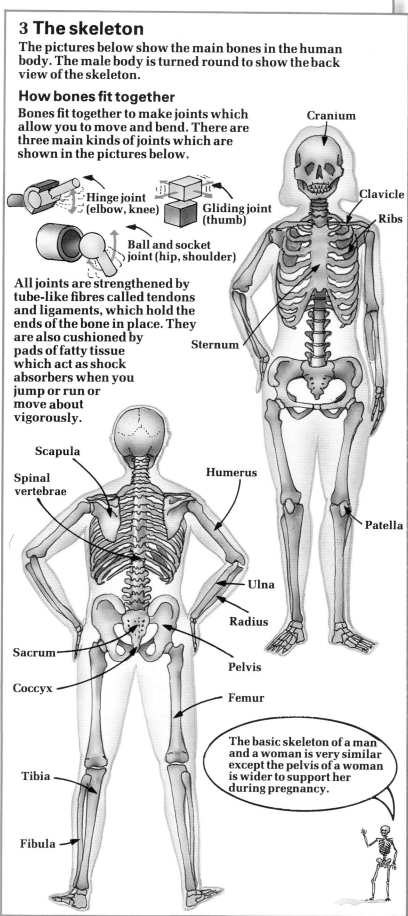

Hinge joint (elbow, knee)
Gliding joint (thumb)
Ball and socket joint (hip, shoulder)

All joints are strengthened by tube-like fibres called tendons and ligaments, which hold the ends of the bone in place. They are also cushioned by pads of fatty tissue which act as shock absorbers when you jump or run or move about vigorously.

Cranium
Clavicle
Ribs
Sternum
Patella

Scapula
Spinal vertebrae
Humerus
Ulna
Radius
Sacrum
Pelvis
Coccyx
Femur
Tibia
Fibula

The basic skeleton of a man and a woman is very similar except the pelvis of a woman is wider to support her during pregnancy.

# Index

First published in 1985 by
Usborne Publishing Ltd, 20,
Garrick Street, London
WC2E 9BJ, England.

Printed in Belgium.

First published in 1985 by Usborne Publishing Ltd, 20 Garrick Street, London WC2E 9BJ, England. Copyright © 1985 Usborne Publishing